# PORTRAIT OF A WOMAN WALKING HOME

T0363082

By the same author:

*where the lost things go* (2017)

*out of emptied cups* (2019)

*the light we cannot see* (2021)

# PORTRAIT OF A WOMAN WALKING HOME

## ANNE CASEY

RECENT
WORK
PRESS

Portrait of a woman walking home
Recent Work Press
Canberra, Australia

Copyright © Anne Casey, 2021

ISBN: 9780645008975 (paperback)

NATIONAL
LIBRARY
OF AUSTRALIA

A catalogue record for this
book is available from the
National Library of Australia

All rights reserved. This book is copyright. Except for private study, research, criticism or reviews as permitted under the Copyright Act, no part of this book may be reproduced, stored in a retrieval system, or transmitted in any form by any means without prior written permission. Enquiries should be addressed to the publisher.

Cover image: © Anne Casey, 2021
Cover design: Recent Work Press
Set by Recent Work Press

recentworkpress.com

SS

*For Mum,*

*always, forever, wherever*

# Contents

Welcome to your Life Cruises self-guided tour [Official transcript]     1
When a woman I've never met asks me to post
a photo of myself feeling beautiful     3
Ingrain     5
Dichotomy     6
Encomium *hymenopus coronatus*     8
Projecting forward     9
Crush     10
Still I rise     12
How to survive an apocalypse     14
Dancing in the moonlight     15
Darkling     16
Patina     17
Over a midnight shore     18
Let me count the ways     19
Vestigial imprint     21
Days like today     23
Consummation of dreams     24
Stations of the Cross     25
A little death I     28
A little death II     29
Red hot sting     30
A great mirror     32
Art Appreciation 101: Earthly Delights     33
Yang mouths to me     35
Midstory     36
On a wing and a prayer     37
Regenesis     39
Desiderata     40
Portrait of a woman walking home     41

Afterword     42

# Welcome to your Life Cruises self-guided tour [Official transcript]

*For Gabrielle*

*Please ensure your personal headset is set to Channel 1 at all times.*

Welcome to       your self-guided       tour       of the State
of Womanhood.    This destination    has been pre-selected for you on a
randomised basis.    You have opted       for the no-frills    version
of this tour.    Please be aware this means    you will incur    additional charges
en route.    We are not responsible       for unforeseen costs    or
for personal losses    damage    injury    or    death    incurred.*

Following a brief passage       through the Strait of Infanthood,
noted for its rosy sunrises and    its perennial flamingo-tinted flora,
we will be approaching our first    drop-off    point.
This is non-optional.       Significant additional expenditure applies.
Please prepare to disembark    for your    overnight adventure
at the    Precipice of Girlhood.    If you have not read    our preparatory    notes
on    local customs,    here is a quick recap:    You do not have an opinion.    If you think
you have an opinion,    it will be summarily refuted.    You will
accept all forms of affection    from random    strangers,    distant relatives,
and 'friends' of    all ages    and persuasions    (no matter how creepy or repugnant).
You will refrain    at all times    from being
loud,    shrill    or argumentative.    (Conduct of this nature is restricted to the Moors
of Shrew,    which destination has been excluded from this tour    for reasons
relating to current litigation.) You are regarded    as inferior    in all matters
related to    logic,    mathematics,    spatial awareness    and physical strength.
You are encouraged to    make significant    purchases    in the gateway giftshop.
The last tender    will depart    at 7 am    sharp.    Please ensure you are    on board.

The highlight       of the next part of your cruise    will be
your visit    to the Capital    of Womanhood.
On the left    you will find    the Plains of Empathy.
Natives of this region    are commonly found    to be friendly.
Caution should be    applied    further to the left    where
radical elements    are known to inhabit the    coastal fringes
as well as heavily wooded    hinterland areas.

Having navigated the         Sound of Education        (with    its   twenty-five
per cent chance      you have      sustained         sexual assault),       you will now
be versed in     fending off      unwanted     physical interactions       to a greater
or lesser extent,  while navigating   obstacles  deliberately
placed in your path.      We recommend          you pause here briefly
and take in          the distant heights          of the Cape of Corporataria.
There you can expect         two thirds pay for like          or higher value work.
Up to forty          per cent of prior         participants    have experienced
sexual harassment  in this location.      Beware low-slung                glass overhead.

In the event         that you         opt         for the side-trip
to the         Geyser Fields of Maternity,         career parking
is available at rear.      Please be aware        that terms and conditions       may change
without notice     in your absence.          A hefty surcharge          is applied
to all late returns. In the event        of your non-return        you may be required to pay
██████████████████      ███████████████████      ████████████████████████**

*We have just received          a tycoon warning.        For your own safety,
please follow         all directions         without question.        Step out of the vehicle.
Interlace your hands      behind your head.        Spread your legs
and await further instructions* ███████████████      ████████████████████**

We hope you have enjoyed          your journey through      the midlands
of      the State of        Womanhood.   Please gather up       all of your resources
as we will shortly     arrive    at the Mines of Menopause.   No appropriate protective
equipment    is available at this time.   Severe conditions   are expected.     We urge
you to take    every precaution   as we navigate [*Static... voice becomes inaudible*].

*Travel Advisory - State of Womanhood:* *Violent and/or fatal assaults have been recorded
in the case of one third of tour participants.*
*\*\*Sections redacted due to ongoing litigation.*

# When a woman I've never met asks me to post a photo of myself feeling beautiful

I turn, frozen at the window, looking out
as lorikeets feast in the shedding trees, bare limbs quivering
in the slightest breeze. A screech pierces the wisp-streaked distance,
shriller than mine before I realised the value of learning—the first teacher
who instructed me in perspective when I told him about the shoe
-print blooming on my pubic bone, the yell
-owing fingerprints budding on my adolescent breasts
and he said *worse things can happen.* He should apply
for a job online, where I learned that moderation means
less-than-average-values and lowest common denominators
after repeatedly opening the window to streaming images of a man-
I've-never-met's private parts in various stages and guises of climax
which does not apparently warrant reprimands—my bad—*worse things can happen*
but I already knew the value of estimating distance, a lesson I had learned
from another teacher in those youthful bruising years—
calculation never my strong suit. In the comments after my
newspaper articles, I learned the immeasurable lengths of free expression,
and its unplumbed depths in the thread at the end of an online forum,
where I finally learned the answer to the question that had stalked me
since fourteen—via a strangling string of invective
like the red mist spraying the windows of the
London double-decker as two girls learned
there is nothing amicable in divisory numbers,
sick words spitting like the blood from their pummelled
noses and split lips, like the screed that had spilled
from the fingertips that pulled the trigger on six
peace-seeking women in a Tallahassee yoga studio—I wonder
if someone stood over their bleeding bodies and informed them
*worse things can happen.* Nobody had so counselled Jyoti Singh
on or before the day that 84 minutes of hell ended her life on a South Delhi bus-ride.

So when a woman I've never met (but have known online for years)
asks me to post a photo of myself feeling beautiful,
though I am aware she went offline several months ago after
protracted harassment, you may understand why I might pause
and close the window—my fingernail catching on the square
of black tape covering the unwanted and

unwelcome lens—as I watch all the rules
I thought I knew and understood
screech into the infinite wisp-streaked blue.

# Ingrain

With a practiced twist, the man on tv
is prising open the fragile mouth,
probing tender flesh unable to resist,
orbs of sunlight string glistening water behind.
Inside the injured tissue, he leaves a small stone—
in time, it will grow a pearly cyst
to smooth over the rough intrusion.

In the jumble of a city flea market once,
I couldn't resist
a string of aged pearls, their soft peach glow
alluring from velvet folds—
I realise now why
no matter how I would twist them,
they would find a way to choke.

How a man's hand can close
over a small mouth, encircle a throat—
unable to resist, injured tissue accepts the stone.
I almost drowned once, refound how words
won't form in the absence of air.
If I could form the words now,
I would tell you how you can drown on dry land.

Never take me to an oyster farm—
all those closed mouths
not forming words under water,
slowly growing over their own small stones.
There are places where a woman can be stoned for failing
to resist a man, her pulped flesh left
to ripen around the stones.

# Dichotomy

She has never learned
not to look
       a wild beast in the eye,
       that she can't fly:
much-bitten, hypernaturally
attracted to light.

She dances to the song
of the ocean breeze,
       takes counsel from clouds,
       whispers with trees,
feasts on lorikeet
shrieks, never sleeps.

I see her through a midnight
skylight—bewitching
       the moon, a galaxy
       at her feet: though I love her,
her attentions are deep
and brief.

*Is there self*
*-ishness*
*in freedom—*
*or is self*
*the last reserve*
*of the free?*

I eat paper, avoid naked
flames, unspool on the
       bathroom floor,
       claw glass
walls, rake
concrete dreams.

I run
with clocks,
       dance to the

>           cloaked
> puppeteer's jerks:
> tick-tock, tick-tock.
>
> She was never yours,
> only part mine:
>           no man's,
>           my island—
> I
> might be her downfall.

# Encomium
## *hymenopus coronatus*

Show me your silken underbelly,
the pearly translucency
of your petal-wings,
wild rose
velvet folds,
moon-bright orbs
pricked with pink,
that small perfect
pout
binding me
to your mercurial
moods.

I know every
skin prickle,
lustrous lair
darkling tier,
a quiver
of hidden
sharp things—

hostage to
all your
thornier
edgings.

# Projecting forward

*For Ali*

I picture us standing just
inside the hall-door,
the nip of a breeze carrying
a spit of rain off the Lee
to eel around our naked ankles.

Hands on hips, the landlady looking a bit
discombobulated, her head bobbing
back and forth like a spectator at Lords,
as she rolls out in broadest Corkonian,
*Was it the wan-room ye wanted?*

Two sets of hazel eyes gaze out at her
from under matching fringes of finest hair—
almost the exact same shade of cow-dung brown—
your head tilting an unspoken Scottish *eh?* at me
and I lamenting that beguiling silenced lilt.

*Two singles next to wan-another sharing a bath,*
she harrumphs leading us past the sacred heart
light glowing red on the wall behind her head
as you roll your eyes behind a lifted shoulder,
a wicked laugh on your parted crimson lips.

# Crush

'In 1910 Dr. Napoleone Burdizzo, an Italian veterinary surgeon, invented the instrument which carries his name... It is used to crush the spermatic cord within the scrotum, resulting in testicular atrophy within about 40 days.'
— Robert Zufall, "Use of Burdizzo Clamp to Crush Vas", *The Journal of Urology*, vol 80, No 3, September 1958

i didn't want him              killed
only crushed              just enough
that he would learn          to exhale
the same stale breath        of despair
he had filled me with        over time

i used to                  picture the scene
hark at the creak of the      shed
door, shiver at          the quiver of
the straw                  shred
caught on              his roped shoulder

the spill of                light pricking
eyes after            all that darkness a
soft                      whimper
warming the chill night      air
his shrivelling truths      laid bare

the truth is i just needed      someone
to crush his tiny mind      but mine was
too                  inconvenient a truth
at the time                  too
easily              brushed aside

unlike this          rancid exhalation in my
ear for all these              years
*"no-one will believe you"*      his
inconvenient truth          always
trumping                  mine

last night i heard          undeniable
creaks in the               dark
shuffles of small feet      the smack of a stick
in a                        soft palm
a gaping grate              of rusted metal

the sounds of               countless
inconvenient                truths
assembling                  for a reckoning

# Still I rise

*After the incomparable Maya Angelou, 1928 – 2014*

You have stalked me down in city streets
with your grubby, prying eyes.
You have rubbed me with your smutty filth,
but still, like dust, I rise.

Did my sexiness arouse you
when I was barely aged thirteen—
when you trailed me with your wanting
gobbing offers so obscene?

Just like storms and like winds,
sure as sunset and sunrise,
as the stars climb the night skies,
still, I'll rise.

When you followed me at eight
years old to display your naked crotch,
did my gaping mouth excite you?
Did you want to make me watch?

Does my indifference offend you—
doesn't make you quite so hard—
'cause I laugh like I've got diamonds
in my own precious heart?

You may slam me with your words;
you may strip me with your eyes;
you may score me with your coarseness;
but still, like your heat, I'll rise.

Does my derisiveness distress you?
Does it come as a surprise—
that I talk like I've got tactics
in the space behind my eyes?

Out of the sheds of men's shamefulness, I rise.
Up from an antiquity of blamefulness, I rise.
I am handed down from Amazons, baptised in their blood—
Daughter of Eve, I'd see you crawling in the mud.

Leaving behind nights of secrets and dread, I rise.
Into a daybreak that's flushed fulsome red, I rise.
Bringing the rage that my fine sisters gave,
I am the cry and the call of the brave.

I rise, I rise, I rise.

# How to survive an apocalypse

*For Owen*

Practice social    media    distancing.
        After every exposure,
        thoroughly wash
        heart (for at least 20 seconds).
Do not hoard
statistics—they have a short shelf life
and offer questionable nourishment.

Wherever possible, dress
inappropriately.
        Seek advice from trees.
Trust the judgment
of animals—
even the tiniest ones.

Practice free flight
in your head.
        Become attracted to light.
Love immoderately.
If in doubt, dance.

# Dancing in the moonlight

It wasn't me he saw
when he held my waist and said
*I will come for you at midnight—*
*listen for the tap, tap, tap at your*
*window.*
It wasn't me entranced at ten.
It wasn't me spooked at sixteen.
It wasn't me able at twenty
to brush him off like all the others.
It wasn't me he promised
to take dancing in the moonlight.
It was the girl who said his name
just like his mother had—
before she tied a tear-stained
luggage-tag to his lapel-button,
blurring the words
no-one would understand
when he landed so far away.
It was the girl he twirled
in the moonlight,
gently holding her waist,
crooning to her the lullaby
his mother had waltzed him to,
notes he hummed
through all the years—
even long after
his mind went dancing.

# Darkling

*For the survivors of the Irish*
*Mother and Baby Homes*

Artemis, protector
of unmarried girls,
where were you
when they howled your name?

Ghosting over shadows
of fates evanesced,
you waxed and waned
while no-one knew

how you'd
let them down.

# Patina

I feel them everywhere,
the ones who left—

the thin girl shivering
in the dark cupboard upstairs
when I reach
to put away the towels;

the strange fruit swinging
inside the wardrobe I avoid,
that wasn't even there
when they came.

They find me
in dark places,
slipping in,
seeking out—

the bride in anglaise lace
all aglow at the altar,
who followed me home
to show her blooming bruises

and her crushed throat.
Such small hands,
so white and hopeful,
wanting to be touched—

gently
yearning for
a soul to see them
for who they would have been.

I feel them everywhere
the ones who left

a piece of themselves behind.

# Over a midnight shore

My last words to her a lie—
    a dark tide lashing
        the broken silver line,

sleet-scattered wind
    rattling dark glass,
        a rasping gasp

as she sprang
    into the frigid gap
        after I told my mother

            she could leave us.

# Let me count the ways

*I:*

*Do you miss her?*

Only when she is off
stood by my father,
shapeshifting his mood.

*Do you miss her?*

Only when she flies to my
brother's side, holding
still to her first-born child.

*Do you miss her?*

Only when she sweeps in
like some changing wind
to bewitch superstitious minds.

*II:*

*Do you miss her?*

Like a small round
stone in the hollow turn
beyond my swollen tongue.

*Do you miss her?*

Like a clinging
vine intertwined in the
cleft of my left ventricle.

*Do you miss her?*

Like the wet black
scratch as a sharp nib
inscribes her name inside my ribs.

*III:*

*Do you miss her?*

Only as far as
ice crystals on the
heights of *Sagarmāthā.*

*Do you miss her?*

Only as deep as
serpentine in the floor
of the Mariana Trench.

*Do you miss her?*

Only as much as
a heart or a lung,
not inasmuch as

I could count the ways.

# Vestigial imprint

How I searched for you everywhere—
fingers buried in the folds
of your nightdress,
pressed to lips,
a trace of you surviving
the unintended
washing.

How I catch you sometimes
in my son's half
-smile, his sideways glance;
how he is unaware of you there
between us in a hug,
my in-breath when I kiss
his head.

How he wriggled
from my lap—knees
grazing the polished boards
as four days before
we blew out
his first candles
around your bedside.

How unconsciously I called
your name, embraced
your lingering
warmth, waves crashing
over and over
below us—the weight
of water
pounding rock

those dark hours as your hand froze
in mine, how still
I search for you
in midnight skies,

eyes cast upwards
palms cupped,
ready to catch

the smallest trace.

# Days like today

I am not old, but I am worn down and frayed at the edges
and I wonder at what age will I say:
Take me away—
let me shed my skin,
release all my atoms.
Let them fall apart still sparking.

Show me the place where they can separate
and stop their spinning:
de-fused, diffuse, drift off;
sink into the moist earth;
seep into the pulsing womb
where bandicoots probe while we sleep—

soil-dappled snouts carrying bits of me
away under the dark branches,
glinting with the watchful eyes of possums,
strung with the spectres of escaped cicadas.
Show me where there will be no more
aching bones and world weariness,

where I can gladly give up my ghost.

# Consummation of dreams

*After Charles Bukowski*

Desiccated cow dungs sunder
and scatter across
grey acres
of
gust-rumpled strand,
skirting pummelled dunes
relenting to relentless tides,
bungled flies flying sideways
in
the whipping wind
to swarm, spit, lick
inside the splintered rim—
a crab's split grin
slipt under,
a single marbled eye staring down
a darkly shrouded sky,
washed up
by
slime-slick seawalls
chafing lashed vessels
trailing spilt rainbows splayed
on the blackening tide
where after
hacking rotting carcasses
from snarled fishing nets—
one of the *lucky*
ones—
I found my purpose
carving out shiny objects
for strangers to peer into,
peck at,
disregard
(a sliver of shucked soul
occasionally glinting
in the discarded shards)—
a penny for your thoughts,
none
mostly.

# Stations of the Cross

Thank Christ as you fly
the coop: battery-packed
          high-rise workstations—
          to duck tailgating
spoilers, facing James
Station, cross past

          the shuttering kiosk edging
          Elizabeth, parry a Coke
can flung by a footloose
bin-looting ibis, dodge Pitt's
          late-blast building-works
          up Park: rubbernecking

the highlit glitter of the quickie
-loan corner pawnbrokers
          to William—and
          the rally, whoop, cry:
early clustering
of the late-shift

          sisterhood: six-foot
          -six Amazons teetering
in their size ten six-inch heels,
stick-thin pins sticking
          out of skin-tight too-high
          way-low Day-Glo,

needle-stick
arms clamping
          clutches stashing
          fossicked scrimpings
for the op, a fix
(alt types

          of pipe dreams);
          unused jimmies
for the shirty johnny-come

-laters, the shadow-shifting
          kerb-skirting kick-seekers—
          wide-berthing the wet

t-shirt pool-comp-touting
Kings Cross Hotel to the welcome
          red glare and stutter
          of the titanic Coke
sign, piles of Lebanese
pizza: one-fifty a giant

          doughy slice—three for
          three
          soakage for the cheap
          drunks—
up the main drag, a heated
squall at the station entrance,
          through the crazed
          tangle of X-rated

neon beacons flashing flesh
temples: not the likeliest
          of shrines to find religion,
          though it restored my faith
for a while in something
higher—that wall

          of muscle taking down the
          off
          -his-face lurching outsider
—with a benevolent,
diamond-crusted smile—
          won unbeknownst for a
          flicker
          of recognition each time

I strode past: limp
-suited, fake snakeskin
          -booted to my knock
          -down bedsitter
where I plugged my ears
to the next-door knocking

-shop, juked junkies
on the back step,
overlooked nightly cop-shows
outside my window
(the right to silence
reserved for the accused)—

that unorthodox
saviour ministering
the illusion of my
incongruous inclusion
until the fetor
and the spilled

body fluids
flushed me out
to higher ground,
where I found
the cost of faith rose
with the postcode.

# A little death I

I have never truly understood
the French term *la petite mort*.
To me, it is so unakin     to dying—
so much more like being hyper-     alive:

like those moments   in movies   when
   the whole world                is paused
while the heroine     moves     through
   the stilled    iridescence    of it all—
water droplets        caught     in sunlit air,
   a floating petal     cupping     golden light,
a hummingbird     suspended     in-flight—
   its magnificent        wings        upheld,
unblurred,   mirrored   alongside   glistening
   stigma folds,     erect stamens     captured
mid-spill     scattering        pollen-powder
   reflecting   in the bright   shining   spheres
of its eyes—        a bursting        constellation
   of inexpressible     beauty   poised on the brink:

liquid, orchid-   scented nectar     trickling
   down the all-   consuming     arc
of an    open-   throated   gasp.

# A little death II

It had sounded so astonishingly simple—
this: *miracle of modern medicine,*
*a complete end to your pain,*
*never have to bleed again*

It had sounded too good to be true—
this: *insert a tiny radio-frequency device*
*through your cervix that will cauterise*
*the inside of your scarred uterus and there*
*will be no more pain.*
But first, right after—
*you can expect some pain.*

So yes, I was expecting the
crushing abdominal cramping
radiating into the back
ache and the bleeding
and the scorched sensation
all through the middle—

but not this: this self-flagellating
*whatthehellwereyouthinking—*
*youarenolongerawom(b)an—*
*youhavekilledthecradlethatheldyourchildren—*
*therewillbenomorechildren* and—
even though you knew all that,
*now* it is real and irreversible,
this new truth borne
inside you.

I had expected the cramping
and bleeding, the burning
and aching, but not this:
this coffin-ship ferrying
a terrible betrayal—this guilt-grief
for the dying thing
I must carry inside me—
*mea culpa, mea culpa, mea maxima culpa*
for

this little death.

# Red hot sting

I felt it all the way—
no pain, just the icky press and separate
as my flesh gave way—
all seven layers—to the
razor-sharp scalpel—
two minutes of cutting,
shaking and trying to breathe,
then the pushing and tugging
and there he was aloft under the light.
My soul reached up to hold him,
all slimed chalky white and bright, bright red.

But black fell down sickly stealing our first meeting,
steel wool filling my throat and ears.
Awakened by my body thrashing
and lashing itself
off the metal table, rebelling against the invasion—
rushed voices, golf stories giving way
to a strange spewing of ccs and pressures
and then I was sailing on a crashing sea,
shuddering uncontrollably,
floating under swimming lights
into an alien lab
planted with human heads strung with wires
atop rolling white waves, watched by small, round, winking eyes.

Embracing him later in a daze,
the red-hot horror of the aftermath mangled up in new love,
nestled next to me in the soft white clouds—
then the rip and scream
and I was the lady sawn in half at the circus,
but without the magic—
clasping the creeping rose at my middle,
a pale-faced aide leaving me holding my two halves together,
trying not to let escape the dark crimson slithering thing I feared might be my liver.
*You've ruptured,* said the nurse from Waterford
what felt like hours later,
letting it slip into a kidney dish—
the paradox lost somewhere in my state of mind.

A nurse from Waterford, turned reiki healer, later told me
I hadn't let go—
that's why I had failed,
in the way it happens—
the switchblade wounds of women's tongues
stinging more than any surgeon's knife,
salved over and over by my children's laughter.
I saw on Facebook years after
that she had a son:
I wonder if she birthed him standing in a field,
then walked away into the sunset clutching her prize,
a cherry-bright stripe glistening on her forehead.

# A great mirror

to augment a new washroom:
no body warning—
two early morning
rose-budded Newton's fruits
giving a little to gravity, but not to me.

Or this rumple-skinned gourd:
umbilical-eyed confronting
Caesar-smiling
reminder of
life's chaliced cycle.

And sometimes I am
wide-eyed child—
grateful, obeisant, silent;
others mother of wonder,
miracle-full shudder

pulled asunder,
ampulla plundered,
disgorged cruet
foundering over
honeydewed cantaloupe—

a fogged-up reflection
of low-hanging fruit
immersed in this daily
over-familiarity
*therapy?*

# Art Appreciation 101: Earthly Delights

I am fourteen; I feel naked, exposed. I close the book, look up, flushed. Suddenly
   shy.
She has been watching me, her face a wry smile. *Finished already?*
I am a small, limp creature held in a leopard's clenched jaws.
I open it again. Furtive as a bird testing the edges of a pond filled with glimpsed
   promises
glistening beneath the surface,
leaping with strange shapes poised to hook you and drag you down. But a
   Christ-like god,
composed, reaches out of the page to calm my shaking hand. If he can look
   unabashed
at the moon-bright beauty of Eve—her nakedness transfixing a prone Adam;
a giraffe stretch fascinated; trees stand unbowed; an elephant uncowed; a
   murmuration
of birds fly blithely by in a distant sky, weaving in and out of orbital orifices
   beneath
the towering spire
of a twisted temple of flesh, *why can't I* cast an innocent, exploring eye?
I am fourteen. Immersed for the first time in the translucent beauty of
   unwrapped skin.
The perfect indifference of this sundry array—*until*—I turn the page.

A rush of seduction. A hand laid just so, dangerously low on a glowing white
   torso.
Palpitating sweetness. *Man. Woman. Bird. Fruit. Succulent. Flesh. Insect.* Field.
Surfaces
rendered fulsome. Ripe. Buttocks. Parted thighs. Riding high. Buck.
Naked. Triumphant. Bearing luscious tributes.
*Blush. Hush, heart racing. Slam. Shut.* Out. Even the angel-fairy beauty:
flower-palace. Organ-ic. Skin-swathed orbs enfolding orchid-like.
Open. Examine. A dance of innocent enrapturement. Strange new worlds
   burgeoning
beneath eager fingertips—*until*—the abrupt bell of a period change. *Take it
   home.*
She is hovering above me. Again. *Read. Absorb. Respond with your own thoughts.*
*I'm not interested in theirs.* An unsheathed figure half-glimpsed
from inside a dark shell. I slam it shut. Feel the weight of it
hidden inside my bag, heft against my hunched shoulder.

I earned an *A minus*, having chosen to largely ignore the third panel. I honestly
    felt
Bosch had done the same. Casting a dark cloak over shame, obscuring the hellish
    claims
of moral punishment in a sliver of lip service observance—Hieronymus and
my high school art teacher
standing side by side to cast aside
my white veil, a miniature replica of the scallop-edged
mantilla my grandmother wore each weekday morning,
to join midstream the murmuration of women
weaving up the main street to eight o'clock mass
under the vast spire that overlooked our tiny seaside town.

# Yang mouths to me

I am prone
to your erectness
gasping
lip to lip
fingertips kissing
nipple
I am captured in
your shado/w/ings
my yin
my magnet/is/ing sun
shade
I am ec/lips/ed
in this
pointillist constellation
in this glimmering greyscale spectrum
your hair w/in/ds/we/pt
over my left breast
Saturn rings
insc/rib/e my blinded eyes
inside
this merged microcosmos
this scattered universe
s/un/burst gathered chaos
of us
I your e/art/hed Apollo
silver quiver below
star:d/us/ted shoulder
Orion's Belt c/inch/ed
at your waist
my felled p/all/our
to your f/all/ing penumbra
molten, moulding, melding
ard/our
as fingertips
kiss nipple
as
lip to lip
gasping
I am pr/one
to y/our erectness

# Midstory

*After Emily Mohn-State*

A babel of lorikeets
tears me from the page
(ironically paper-bound)
where—while watching her
baby daughter—the poet is trying
to grow a tree by not looking
at her iPhone; a clatter
of wattle birds
clamours nearby for top spot,
the highest surfing
the teeter-totter as would-be
usurpers swoop and rush.

*A flurry of miners*
*lancing through—*

a dog barking somewhere down
below in the gully, not mine
who is sitting up beside me
adrift in our treetop bower
sniffing the late afternoon
faux-autumn air
for answers
to unasked questions,
my sons' voices rising
from the neighbour's garden
as I take up my iPhone
to grow a small poem.

# On a wing and a prayer

Tiny star twinkling in the mid-morning sun,
      minute emissary
      expelled from clustered time,
set adrift to witness the callistemon calyx
wither and die
      so close to fertile ground;

parachuting past the brush turkeys
      scruffling and scrounging—
      irresistible instinct pressing them
into early spring service—
beneath the branches where
      gaggles of galahs cackle and gorge,

indifferent to their albino cousin's difference,
      his anaemic peculiarity obscured
      by whatever kinship lies beneath;
drifting in the neverspace,
solitary voyager
      cast out of cosy consort;

past the pair of kookaburras
      silently surveying their domain,
      resolutely unperturbed
by the noisy miners with their bombing raids—
archly arrowed,
      determined to harangue;

yearning for the warm earth—
      to be swallowed up shallowly—
      thirsting for the bright, soft rain
to swell and burst you
into a new magnificence,
      to rise in glorious reflection

and adorn the morning
with your golden crown;
tiny star
floating on a spring breeze
aching to arrive,
to be reborn,

adrift alone.

# Regenesis

If ever you find yourself
in a place of unusual incongruity,
at odds with someone, something
or other, the whole universe, or even
just yourself,
take the time
to remember
when everything was grey
and all over the world
people were dying
of one thing
or another
(but mostly that one thing)
—a disappearing as if
into an abyss:
a great grey abscess
which was an absence
and how: when it became clear,
a wave, small at first
then swelling to a
tremendous roar
filled the whole world
with the understanding
and that was called
the end of times
because after it
came the beginning:
and the world
was made new,
filled
with that
essential
that had
once been

so greatly
missing

if only we had realised
sooner

## Desiderata

A scattering of blue skies,
a pocketful of hope,
the love of one good soul,
no regrets,
the promise of a world made miraculously less cruel for my children,
easy company,
the smell of the sea—

all that I desire
on the long walk home.

# Portrait of a woman walking home

I like the way the sinking sun slips a golden aureole around you on that last straight stretch
of twilit street just before you round the corner falling suddenly under the towering
penumbra of these deserted edifices so recently bustling with workers exiting—
their veins visibly throbbing with concerns of the day—now soaring in
silence stripped of activity as if subjected to the unexpected descent
of some cataclysmic event while you were finishing up that last
pile dropped off by your manager with such urgency it needed
completing before his return tomorrow morning and though
you held up your end, now finding despite your own best
instincts you are wandering halo-less—alone—down this
dusk-lit street clutching your bag against a skateboarder
shooting out from under a gaping facade like that time
with the razor-blade-wielding trio you inexplicably
chased and though you escaped unharmed there
is always that scar of doubt lingering alongside
the stomach-churning whispers and worse—
the still-felt imprints—but there is no
escaping the current situation
and that really is such
a nice pair
of sheer

black stockings
perfectly paired with
those moderate heels showing
off your finely toned calves your hem
gliding just above the delicately curved backs
of your knees stirring in unison with the soft waves
around your raised but ever-so-slight shoulders and you
know though you do your prescribed daily workout with
just enough resistance you will never quite muster the power
you would need and it takes a certain set of eyes to realise on
your approach through the now-profound dusk to the welcome
arc of each lamppost that your silky blouse illuminates so precisely
from behind one can pick out the exact lines of your body moving so
fluidly within its satiny folds sashaying with the swing of your hips though
I know you are making extreme efforts to lessen the sway there is a certain gait
you cannot ameliorate in this corporate get-up—skirt over heels over female pelvis
and it is so obviously more-than-a-little inadvisable for you to have placed yourself in
this delicate position where you might be seen to provoke a certain reaction in an onlooker
of a particular disposition—it being late and you quite clearly under-dressed for the hour and
with every breath you take wondering why it is                    we have to watch

ourselves like this.

# Afterword

You ask me what this book is about. And I tell you *It's complicated*. I am a woman. And this book is about being me. It's about being a woman. It could be about another woman. Many women. Any woman? Maybe. And so. *It's complicated*. It is complicated. In the way that being any second class citizen. Is complicated. And in other ways too. It's complicated. In the way that being treated differently because of the random. Nature. Of your physicality is complicated. It's complicated. Because. Half the world is made up. Of people like me. And not like me. It's complicated because. Mostly we pretend. Everything is okay. Most of the time. And sometimes some of the time. When really it's not. It's complicated. In the way that you spend most of your life. Trying to forget. And then someone shouts *Me too!* from a rooftop. And more voices join her. And then you hear your own voice. And it is outraged. And hopeful. And relieved. And horrified. And fearful. (All over again.) All at the same time. It's complicated because. It's not all bad. It's also about being. A mother. A daughter. A friend. A lover. A warrior (even if that word embarrasses you when you use it about yourself). A person whose body is at war. With itself. With the world. With her. It's about being. An ageing failed rockstar. A dreamer. (Just kidding about the rockstar part.) It's about love, lust, loss and the delicate art of keeping it together. Even in your broken moments. So yeah. *It's complicated*. And sometimes. Sometimes. It is. Unimaginably. Beautiful.

# Notes

**'When a woman I've never met asks me to post a photo of myself feeling beautiful'**: On 20 March 2020, four men were executed for the brutal gang rape and murder of 23-year-old student, Jyoti Singh in New Delhi, a case that highlighted globally the shocking rates of sexual assault in India.

**'Encomium hymenopus coronatus'**: *Hymenopus coronatus* is the scientific name for the (walking) flower mantis or (pink) orchid mantis.

**'Darkling'**: In 2017 the bodies of 800 babies were discovered in a septic tank under one of Ireland's now infamous Mother and Baby Homes. These were institutions all over Ireland where tens of thousands of young women were incarcerated, under harsh conditions, for the sole reason that they were unmarried and pregnant. Survivors have come forward to share their harrowing stories. It is a horrifying history of illegal adoptions, illicit vaccine trials and unmarked mass graves. The last of these homes closed its doors in 1996. In January 2021, the Prime Minister of Ireland issued a public apology following the shocking report by an official inquiry into fourteen of the homes.

**'Let me count the ways'**:
1. The title for this poem originates from a line in the 43rd sonnet of a collection of love sonnets written by Elizabeth Barrett Browning.
2. *Sagarmāthā* meaning "Peak of Heaven" is the Sanskrit name for Mount Everest.

**'A little death I'**: *La petite mort*, meaning "the little death", is the French term for orgasm.

**'Art Appreciation 101: Earthly Delights'** is an ekphrastic poem in three parts inspired by the poet's first experience of the three-panelled artwork entitled *The Garden of Earthly Delights* by Hieronymus Bosch.

**'Yang mouths to me'** is an ekphrastic poem responding to *The photographer's shadow (Olive Cotton and Max Dupain)*, c. 1935 (printed 1999) by Olive Cotton, National Portrait Gallery, Canberra, ACT, Australia.)

**'Midstory'** was written while reading the poem 'Landscape with iPhone' by Emily Mohn-State in *New Ohio Review*, Issue 25 2019.

# Acknowledgments

My heartfelt gratitude to Shane Strange and his trusty team of poetry crusaders at Recent Work Press for welcoming me into the fold with this book. Thank you for the tireless work you do in bringing poetry into the world.

Sincere thanks to the editors of the following publications in which versions of some poems from this book were first published: *The Irish Times*, *Into the Void Magazine*, *Barzakh* (Albany, State University of New York, USA), *The Australian Showcase Edition* of *The Enchanting Verses*, *The Blue Nib*, *ROPES*, *Abridged 0 - 58: Kassandra*, *Verity La*, *HUSK Magazine*, *Autonomy* anthology (New Binary Press 2018), *where the lost things go* (Salmon Poetry 2017), *out of emptied cups* (Salmon Poetry 2019), *Live Encounters*, *Noir Nation Issue No 9 2020*, *Pratik: A Magazine of Contemporary Writing, XVI, 1 Celebrating Irish Muse November 2019*, *Borderless* (Recent Work Press 2021), *Not Very Quiet* Issue 7 'Memoir', and *Other Terrain* (Swinburne University Melbourne).

Thank you to everyone who has purchased, read, and taken the time to respond to my poetry, or indeed poetry anywhere.

## Awards and recognition for poems in this book

'Welcome to your Life Cruises self-guided tour [Official transcript]' was awarded 1st Place in the *Into the Void Poetry Prize 2020* (Canada).

'When a woman I've never met asks me to post a photo of myself feeling beautiful' was longlisted for *The Plough Prize 2019* (UK).

'Still I Rise' won 3rd Prize in the *Women's National Book Association* (USA) *Annual Writing Contest 2018*.

'Still I rise', 'Portrait of a woman walking home' and 'Crush' were shortlisted for the *Overton Poetry Prize 2018* (UK).

'Still I rise' was shortlisted and awarded Special Mention in the *Aryamati Poetry Prize 2019* (UK).

'A great mirror' was a Finalist in the *Summer Literary Series 2018 Fiction & Poetry Contest* (Canada).

'Yang mouths to me' was longlisted for the *Palette Poetry – The Emerging Poet Prize 2020* (USA).

'Projecting forward' was Commended in the *Roscommon County Library Poetry Competition 2018* (Ireland).

# About the Author

Originally from the west of Ireland and living in Sydney, Anne Casey is an award-winning poet/writer and author of three critically acclaimed poetry collections—*where the lost things go* (Salmon Poetry 2017), *out of emptied cups* (Salmon Poetry 2019) and *the light we cannot see* (Salmon Poetry 2021). She has worked for 30 years as a journalist, magazine editor, media communications director and legal author. Senior Poetry Editor of *Other Terrain* and *Backstory* literary journals (Swinburne University, Melbourne) from 2017-2020, she has served on numerous editorial advisory boards.

Anne's writing and poetry are widely published internationally and rank in leading national daily newspaper, *The Irish Times'* Most-Read.

She has won/shortlisted for poetry prizes in Ireland, Northern Ireland, the USA, the UK, Canada, Hong Kong and Australia – including *the American Writers Review Competition 2021, ACU Prize for Poetry, Henry Lawson Poetry Competition, Women's National Book Association of USA Poetry Competition, The Plough Prize, Atlanta Review International Poetry Contest, 25th Annual Melbourne Poets Union International Poetry Competition, Hennessy New Irish Writing, Cúirt International Poetry Prize, Overton Poetry Prize, Bedford International Writing Competition, Tom Collins Poetry Prize* and *Fellowship of Australian Writers Queensland Literary Competition.*

Anne's poems feature internationally in newspapers, magazines, journals, anthologies, podcasts, music albums, stage shows and art exhibitions –*The Irish Poetry Reading Archive* (James Joyce Library, UCD), *The Irish Times, The Canberra Times, Australian Poetry Anthology, Griffith Review, American Writers Review, Atlanta Review, Beltway Poetry Quarterly, Tahoma Literary Review, Quiddity, Entropy, The Murmur House, Barzakh* (State University of New York), *Connecticut River Review, The Stony Thursday Book, Westerly Magazine* and *Cordite Poetry Review* among many others.

Anne holds a Law Degree from University College Dublin and qualifications in Media Communications from the Technological University Dublin (Dublin Institute of Technology). She is undertaking a PhD at the University of Technology Sydney, supported by an Australian Government Research Training Program Scholarship.

Website: anne-casey.com. Social media: @1annecasey.

Printed in Australia
Ingram Content Group Australia Pty Ltd
AUHW020929220224
390784AU00002B/45